Placebo Paradox

When I was twelve, I found a note attached to a fallen balloon.

It read,

"My Wish -

For the human race to realize and reverse the trends of greed, avarice, apathy, sloth, and self-gratification, so my children can grow up in a world better than the one we are creating for them now."

This book is for the person who wrote this note, and everybody else with a wish.

The colors changed around us, and the heart crushing, soul stealing, eye watering pain came in later because I hadn't said it yet. I eventually did, but the problem in the end was that you had forgotten how to. Autumn is my favorite season because the leaves fall and they are so beautiful as they delicately glide onto the partially frozen earth below. I remember our first walk in autumn, when you stepped on a fiery orange leaf and it made that satisfying crunch. On that September day, I smiled, kept, and craved the sound, not knowing that next autumn I would hear the same crunching sensation coming from my heart.

He will spend the days without me, drowning in miles and maps and distance. The nights would not be spent together even though I would want them to be. There is something addictive in feeling sorry for yourself.

The reason girls seem so bipolar and confusing is because we all want a happy medium that doesn't actually exist.

The sea sings and the fog slows my breathing. I glance over to my side where silver fish wade and green seaweed dances. A seagull flies overhead and a wave splashes at my feet, cold and clammy. How was I supposed to feel when it all changed for good?

You always say that you can read my mind but if this is true then you should be ashamed of yourself for not getting me some help

You would think that I would hate the pretty girl.
I don't.
I just want her dead.
No, not dead. Just gone, from me at least.
I didn't want to see her blonde hair,
styled perfectly with it's blue tips. It reminded me of
how self-centered she is.
I didn't need to see her lips, shaped like geometrical
diamonds layered perfectly in a pucker, caked with
lipstick. It made me remember how she never told the
truth.
I was sick of her skinny, bony frame. It made me think
of how she gave her body away so easily.
I soon forgot the color of her eyes, wide like quarters
when she wasn't crying. She denied that too.
The only feature of hers that I cared for was her
ex-lover.
Mine now.

my ribcage is collapsing on itself and I must write this quick for I may soon die or kill myself or drown in my own sadness and I just want someone who will dry my tears even at the darkest of hours

How dare you tell her that you cared too much when you never even gave a shit about us.

I knew deep down inside that there was nothing that I could do or say to make him stay with me, but that didn't keep me from fighting for him.

I tried everything that I could to get the image off of my mind, but it's burned into my skull. I want these pictures to move out of my brain but they won't go away and I can't sleep with them in there.

I remember the look in your eyes, the way they glassed over themselves and how your lips drew a chapped line. I remember how my voice shook when I told you that I thought I was being emotionally abused by you. You were silent at first, it was probably only for a split second but it felt like hours in my heart, which was beating out of my chest. Your throat then began to spew venom and even though I was being intoxicated by your abuse, I stayed because I loved you.

It is scary that I got to the point where I blamed myself for being the reason why you looked both ways before you kissed me.

I'm insane, that's what. I want what is possible but what can't possibly happen. I put too much pressure on single moments and that is why I will always be disappointed.

Your name.

I like the sound.

The word.

I want to say it over and over again,

so I can feel this overwhelmingly thrilling sensation in my chest.

Your name.

The name feels safe in my mouth when I say it,

pronounce it,

think it,

sing it,

mouth it,

whisper it,

yell it,

laugh it.

I love it.

Your name.

It's like the water that keeps a flower growing, the air that keeps flowing through my lungs.

I say your name and then I feel like everything will be okay.

I feel like I've found my place,

like someone has finally found the key to my heart.

It is wonderful and so fabulous to be in love. But it is a scary thought that you could just pack your bags and leave me with all the memories. And it terrifies me so much that you, one person, one soul, my love, have complete and utter power to vanish, ultimately leaving me with shocking pain and sorrow. But I need to trust that you won't destroy me.

Now I'm pressing a loaded gun into your soft palm. Now I'm handing you cold, heavy bullets. Now I'm whispering words of inspiration into your ears, giving you new ideas on different ways to kill me. And now I'm trusting that you will never pull the trigger.

Sometimes,
with glitter and sequins,
you can make someone
look a thousand times better
than they will ever be.
And sometimes,
even you will be fooled
by your own art.

You told me that love is like cross country and I thought that that analogy was so cute until it was 3 am and I remembered that all races have finish lines and all cross meets have winners. And you, well, you ran a five minute mile.

the thorn protects the rose

The last person to break my heart was myself because I am going to live with myself for the rest of my life and I can't help but see this as a curse.

Dear self,

I forgive you for breaking my heart and that is why now we are getting help. I want to make things right between us.

Kind regards,
me

That day in the woods,
With your arm around me.
So beautiful and perfect.
It was one of those little things that you look back at
later on and realize that it was actually a big thing.

Later on, though, I forgot.

When people ask if your acts are purposeful, tell them that nothing in literature happens on accident. When they tell you that not everything in life is literature, respond with, "not if I am writing all of this down."

Relationships are like disposable cameras.
You are given something that you can take
pictures with, but you are not yet aware of what you
will photograph. You can use up the camera, but you
only have a limited number of shots you can take
before it's too late. You can take your time with things
and make the camera last. You can get the pictures
developed later, too. Or you can toss it away,
undeveloped and half-used, still able to be given a
second chance but thrown away before we really knew
what we had.

This isn't going to be easy, it's going to be extremely
difficult at times. Relationships, like this disposable
camera, take work in order to see results. You either do
the work or you get out.

The harsh reality is that there are many more cameras
to use.

And there are many more relationships to be in.
It all depends on your angle,
your way of looking at things.

I wish that we will always be the crazy stupid sleepless lovesick fools that we are right now. I wish that we will always love each other in this powerful manor.

When people are unkind, it is because their demons have taken control over them.

I am sorry that you are so possessed.

If you're happy again,
who cares how long it took?

I lost my innocence when the heartbroken thirteen year old me covered myself in blankets, sobbing on my bed, unable to sleep or eat. When I started scratching the paint off of my walls. My floor was scattered with crumpled up used tissues and my heart still ripped into shreds when June turned into July and July turned into August.

You were wise and gentle with your words and thoughts and comfort. You were calm but weren't afraid to throw punches. Your bubbly laugh would echo through the walls of my house at 2 am and I would smile sweetly at you and want to move myself closer to you in any way I could. I wanted to touch every part of your body and spirit. I knew that if I ever got to kiss a woman like you then I would be the luckiest woman alive. I wanted into you. Your skin. Your pants. Your heart. The world was a cold thunderstorm and you were a toasty and cozy house and I was banging on the windows louder and louder until, when I thought the door would open, the lights just shut off.

-not all houses are homes

When we hold hands, our hearts become one. If we could get everybody in the world to hold hands at once, we would all find peace.

Everyone thinks that they feel things deeper than others.
Everyone thinks that they're something special.
But are we just self-centered, recycled copies born off of coincidences and happenstance who are hoping and praying that we will be the ones who end up different?

Loving you was like laughing at a joke that wasn't funny.

Respect is earned, not given.
Love is given, not earned.

People will leave you when you are in the time of most need and expect you to be okay with that.

she says
that she
is a paradox
but this
is only because
she is so transparent
to everyone
except
for herself.

Learn, love, explore, and discover the difference between existing and living.

she was the type of girl that you only hear about in songs

He doesn't like leaving things unsaid so he's never the first one to hang up the phone.

Our friendship always gave me hope, even when I wanted to die. We burned photographs of bad memories but I didn't know that in five months I'd be taking one last look at a photo of us before tossing it into the flames to become nothing but ashes and a faint memory. I watched the picture burn, that black and white photo of us smiling so big in October in the way that you could tell that we never knew of that sunken feeling inside of your chest when your best friend and true love tells you that they just can't handle you anymore.

Sometimes I try to imagine all of the pictures that I was accidentally in the background of.

Or wonder what it would be like to count the amount of lost money in the world.

Or I think of if I could measure the amount of all the tears in the world that have been cried in secret.

Or the number of suicides that could have been prevented by a single phone call.

Or how many people there would be in the world if everyone who had ever attempted suicide was actually successful.

Or how many lives and families would be put back together if suicide was an impossible task.

Or how many faces would be glowing if suicide simply did not exist.

Or how many people would have been hurt if I was successful in suicide.

But I do not wonder how to commit suicide without hurting anybody.

Because I already know the answer to this question.

How do you kill yourself without hurting anybody?
Don't.

His tears seeped through the telephone line like an unexpected thunderstorm. It rained that day. A freezing rain, the droplets trapped in air and time until they came crashing down to the ground below. Maybe that's how his heart felt, with her chilly, rough hands squeezing their way around all feeling he had ever known. But his eyes darted away, her power thawed, her thunder silenced. He soon saw the rainbow after the prolonged pouring stopped, but that was the day he understood why terrible storms are named after people.

He whispers words to me that I actually want to hear. Deep down in my desires, darkened by an abusive one, this boy brings my light back out. He tells me how beautiful he finds me as he kisses me slowly, stopping to admire the petals before picking the flower. He takes the time to smell the roses, not to be polite, but because I am his favorite scent.

I have learned to be humble because we all end up
underground somehow

Remember that love cannot be taught, but it is something that comes naturally.
And if you have to learn how to love him, then you don't.

They say that the past is the past but how am I supposed to forgive you for trying to take the stars out of my sky?

If you kiss me, I will hold you forever.
If you leave me, I will pull down the sun.
If you stay with me, nothing will ever hurt again.

I am so sorry that I stole him from you but when I put him in my pocket and left your store, the alarms did not go off.

Infatuation fades.
Love is eternal.

I want to walk right up to you and ask why it is that you hate me so much. How can you stand silently just to watch me crumble into bits of nothing by the things that you meaninglessly utter? I want to ask why you formulate hatred in your mind to spew at me, or if it just comes out without your mind's approval first.

But then I remember that you never even got the chance to know me.

Then I begin to understand that there is a fine line between feeling nothing and feeling hate.

You told me that you'd be back, but in a different form.
And I feel like I'm not looking hard enough.
But I also know that there are things out there that I
don't know of and there are people living, who I've
never even met.
I told you that I'm never satisfied.
The truth is, I'm just too scared to settle.

I know that
an evil witch
put you under
a lifelong spell
but please
don't let
your heart
explode.

You gave me the feeling that I used to get in my fingers as a child when it was cold out and I forgot to wear mittens.

My knuckles would tense up and my entire hand would soon go completely numb from the freezing cold.

But then I would go inside after playing in the snow, and I'd feel the heat of the house and suddenly my fingers were so cold that they were warm, and so warm that they were cold, wrapped up in a haze of tingling confusion.

This is what you did to my heart.

But because of you I have learned a few things;

That sometimes people will jump out of planes without parachutes if they are unconvincingly and unknowingly promised a happily ever after.

And sometimes boys enter the bodies of girls they shouldn't.

And sometimes we lie to hide things that we wish did not happen, like if we refuse to acknowledge them then they do not exist.

And sometimes there are occurrences that don't make any sense, but we must cope with them anyways.

And sometimes it snows in May.

My dad waves at every stranger he sees when he's driving.
He always says,
"You never know if that person really needed that today."

Never in my life have I wished that I could stop thinking, until I met you.

Before the moon melts
and the stars fade away
or the love of your life
changes her mind one day,
You must decide to take the chance
of choosing to leave or stay.

I loved you before you were even mine. I should have known from the way you looked at her, so bored and impatient and blank, I should have known that you were looking at me.

The way you smiled at me when we were alone, how your eyes would light up when you talked about something you were fond of.

You weren't smiling that night.

Fast forward to a year later when I was the old her and who I used to be was somebody else.

thunderstorms washing away

the memories

before my eyes

like the tears

I never cried

They told me that the cuts that didn't bleed didn't count.
They didn't understand that I still envision slashes on my wrists.
They told me that if I couldn't bring myself to create them, then I wasn't worthy of that kind of sadness.

Home isn't a location. It's the feeling you get when you kiss the right person.

mental health issues,
big or small,
should never
be taken lightly
or laughed at
or brushed aside
because
what an awful feeling
this is,
wanting to die
yet holding on for dear life
at the exact same time

My emotions are your emotions.
But my heart is not your heart.

Show her off or let someone else do it.

I do not believe that everything happens for a reason. But I do believe that everything that does happen teaches you something.

When you love and see the good in everything.
When you love and don't look back.
When you love and dive in head first.
When you love and you don't care what anybody thinks.
When you love and have no regrets.

The rain cannot remember me.
The air must drown me.
The sea will carry me home.

catch me
when I fall
from the overdose
of your presence,
I feel butterflies
when you are around

I am broken there.
You are fixed now.
We are whole forever.

nothing

haunts

us

like

the

parties

we

weren't

invited

to

I promise you that I will kiss your scars every night before we go to sleep so then you will see that sweetness can come from even the worst kinds of pain.

I wish to someday see you again, or at least hear directly from you.

(I would throw this out a window but I know you've already read it)

When you dull your lipstick, try not to dull your spirit.

When there is nothing but sea, humans will grow fins, gills, and tails, and we will all learn how to swim.

When you first meet him, just breathe.
Remember to feel your heartbeat.
When you fall in love with him, just breathe.
Remember to regulate your heartbeat.
When he leaves you, just breathe.
Remember to keep your heartbeat.

I know I must clean my brain for demons so my head will not explode.

I know I must work hard to not hate myself for what I am not.

I know I must be patient with my art and my creative process.

It is comforting and haunting to know that every day is
someone's best day,
someone's worst day,
someone's first day,
someone's last day,
and someone's typical day.

I feel like if I am ever half as happy as I was when I first kissed you, I will die with more experience of happiness in my heart than everyone in all of existence combined.

I wrap barbed wire around my brain, to keep the anxiety from going too far. I protect my heart with all my might because I don't want the anxiety to poison it like it did before.

You only get one heart.

the ghosts told me that it's too soon to be early

She says that she'll never be surprised.
Surprise her anyways.
She says that she's not very hungry.
Make sure she eats.
She says she likes adventure, so take her on one.
She says that she loves to take photographs.
Do not hesitate when you see her pointing a camera your way.
She says that her anxiety is too strong.
Hold her until the attack passes through.
She says that she hates her laugh.
Tell her millions of your lame jokes and always tickle her.
She says that she's hard to love.
Love her anyways.

how can I
   expect you
      to love me
         when I don't
            even love myself

The first time I fell in love, I did not pay attention to the sky. My tunnel vision and anxiety caused me to only catch brief glimpses. After he left me, I only ever saw the sky. Hoping at first that he would come back, but soon making new wishes on falling stars that the planets would align and I would be given someone new. I eventually was presented with a new sky and what was a constant thunderstorm of an eternal night became a warm evening with peachy clouds and soft pink lights.

When someone touches my hair, I hear my mother telling me stories of her dreams of a past life.

When someone hides their face, I hear the voice that used to be inside my head, holding me back from my dreams.

When someone ignores me, I hear a cracking sensation coming from my chest, feeling like I don't deserve the dreams that I have.

When someone smiles, I hear the world living another day. Because one dream coming true is enough hope for all of humanity.

As he hugged me for the last time, I could feel his weighty heart beating, adding a slight heaviness to the air.

If I were a star, I would fall next to the person that needed it.

The girl who hasn't eaten in two days, dizzy with self-hatred and doubt.

The writer that hasn't picked up a pen in four months, the writers block so thick, he cannot see.

The woman who just received the news that her mother lost her battle to cancer earlier this morning.

The boy who really wants out of his geometry exam.

The boy who just got kicked out of the house for simply wanting to kiss other boys.

The runner who completed her first 5K with a time that she didn't think she could ever run.

If I were a star, I would fall next to the person who needed it.

Everybody needs it at some point.

I looked at the love of my life and wondered what I had become.

We live in the past to the point where we do not exist.

We go out to dinner as a family and share stories that have been told a thousand times.

The food we consume is the only thing still keeping us here.

It makes me wonder if there are any more memories to be made if we are not living in the present.

I shed blood for the first time yesterday and now all I can see today are the ghosts dripping out of my wounds and intoxicating the air that I am breathing and going back inside of me again

-vicious cycle

Keep a notebook under your pillow so then on the days when it's too hard to get out of bed, you can write down a giant list of every question that you will never find the answers to.

always chase your dreams
from the moment I kissed you, I knew
you are my dream

He says, "I want you."
Sunflowers grow around my hip bones, all the way around my waist.

He says, "I understand you."
Lilacs grow up my throat and out of my mouth.

He says, "I love you."
Red and pink roses grow around my heart, cradling it softly.

He says, "I need you."
I would be given strong oak trees for arms.

He says, "I miss you."
Small thorn branches grow up the back of my spine.

but

how

can

I

be

recognized

for

my

success

when

there

is

nobody

there

On this rainy,
droopy,
gloomy day,
I look out my window and the tears of the angels bleed
out of the sky and drip onto my windowpane.
And I think about the way I used to sit here and think
about you
and how you made me feel
and how now
we mean nothing to each other

and I am so sorry to everyone that I grew apart from
and pushed away just so I could get closer to him

Pain is something that we have no control over. What we can control, though, is suffering.

We get over people,
we do not get over what people do to us.
We forget what people say,
we do not forget how people make us feel.

Being human is magic.
A piece of paper can either be a love note or a hand grenade, depending on your mood.

If everything in life is on a spectrum, then nothing is definite.

If everything in life is open to interpretation, then there are no rules.

If everything in life is as you perceive it, then there are no questions to be asked.

I always look at the stars when I really miss him. They remind me that he's never too far away because we're both under the same stars.

We are all monsters in some shape or form, just hidden underneath our costumes.

Every last noise you made was music to my ears. I want to download your noises and arrange them into a playlist and put them on repeat.

There is no such thing as pleasing everyone. But there is such thing as finding someone who is worth more than that.

You told me that the only way you would ever leave me was through death.

I remember your lifeless eyes six months later when you told me that you weren't coming back.

After he leaves you,
When you say his name, it will sound stupid in your mouth.
But if you swallow your words, they will burn going down.

Everything is uglier up close.
Once you find something that isn't, keep it.

If every relationship is different, then there is no right or wrong way to start one.

It terrifies me to know how much humans are capable of doing. It terrifies me even more to not know.

The surface becomes farther away,
and the sea is inside of me.
I'm full of sea.
Inside my veins the salt runs through.
My eyes are green,
no longer blue.
My lungs are soaked,
drenched with thick sea foam.

The messages that you all tried to send to me were scattered. We need to pick up the pieces.

The way people treat you is a direct reflection of the way you treat yourself.

When I kiss you, I feel firework explosions in my chest. It reminds me of the fourth of July when there's a colorful sky and with every crack and sizzle heard a new kind of energy is formed. I love you more and more every time I kiss you.

The day that you stop giving strangers the benefit of the doubt is the day that your spirit dies.

When bad things happen, they only stay bad if you allow them to. Never give into the bad, always work harder to correct things, and never stop until you have the control over it. The negative is the easy part. When great things happen, and your reaction to it will make the difference in your life. You need to understand how lucky you are and be smart enough to be humbled by your great moments.

-in the words of my father

I feel as though
I am at war
with myself
sometimes,
because
I fall
in love
with the moon
every night.

If you have ever left me, I hope that it was because you were in search of something better.
And if this is the case, I hope you have found it.

She
licked
the
sugar
off
of
his
lips
and
tasted
poison

It is complex,
but true,
that I did not
need to like you
in order
to love you.

It doesn't take that much effort to make a person's day, but what you say can affect them for the rest of their life.

I feel like I'm trapped as the victim in a horror film
inside of my own brain
and there is no escape
except self destruction

I would love to look in the mirror and say something that would make me instantly fall in love with myself

People who say that they don't believe in love just haven't found the right person yet.

Do you believe that nothing is as good or bad as it seems?

Do we all live in an area of grey?

Who you love is not a choice.
How you love them is.

Some people don't deserve to be left on good terms.

Don't feel like you have to go with the flow, and never say *maybe* if you really mean *no*.

Many of us would be zombies if one day the universe decided that from this point on, people would lose an hour of sleep for every tear that they caused others to cry.

Write.

Because your heart will bleed onto the pages until it is ready to feel again.

Acknowledgements

First and most importantly, thank you mom and dad for motivating me to read since a young age, and for giving me a wide variety of books to choose from. Your nonstop love and support will eternally live inside of me.

Lottie, thanks for having my back through everything, just like a good sister should. Also, I would not be where I am today without your constructive criticism about everything in my daily life, rant sessions, and intense opinions. Your strong mind and determination has given me loads of inspiration for writing.

Grandma Foote, thank you for always encouraging me to follow my dreams in order to get exactly what I want out of life. I am grateful for your huge role in my life today, even though you have been gone for five years.

Thank you to my good friend, Paige, for designing the cover of my book. This was a small task on your part, but you really helped capture the exact vibe that I wanted.

Also, I can't forget my boyfriend, Skylar, for inspiring me to take this huge leap into pursuing my dream. You've truly shown me that anything is possible once you believe in yourself...Thank you for believing in me.

I must end this with recognizing the people who do not need to be named:

To the ones who have left me or I have left behind; thank you for giving me melancholy feelings that I would one day turn into poetry.

And the ones who continue to be close to my heart; I appreciate the friendship, positivity, and encouragement that has been given to me by each and every one of you.

You all know who you are.